To Alysha
Dec' 2002
Lots of Love
Gran ~ Grandpa
x x

Mary

Joseph

Angel

Donkey

Innkeeper

The Story of
Jesus

Illustrated by Chris Rothero

It's fun to Read Along

Here's what you do –

These pictures are some of the characters and things the story tells about. Let the child to whom you are reading SEE and SAY them.

Then, as you read the story text and come to a picture instead of a word, pause and point to the picture for your listener to SEE and SAY.

You'll be amazed at how quickly children catch on and enjoy participating in the story telling.

ISBN 1-84135-034-6

Copyright © 1992 Award Publications Limited

First published 1992
This edition first published 2000

Published by Award Publications Limited,
1st Floor, 27 Longford Street, London NW1 3DZ

Printed in Belgium

Manger

Wise Men

Palms

Fishes

Jesus

King

Camels

THE STORY OF JESUS

Once, long ago, a gentle young girl

called  was at home in

Nazareth when an  visited her.

The 's name was Gabriel and

he told  that God had sent

him. "You will have a ," the

 said. "His name will be Jesus,

Son of God."

 was engaged to marry a

carpenter who lived in the same

town. His name was  and after

they were married  liked to

watch  at work.  might

be busy making a  or mending

a wooden for a cart but he

always had time for

 was soon to have her

 and  was very worried

when he heard that he must take

 to Bethlehem. "We must all

go," he said, "to be counted. The

 commands it."

"I will get some food ready for the

journey,"  said.

When everything was ready they

set out,  seated on a  .

What crowds there were in

Bethlehem! It was growing dark and

 had still not found a room.

He could see how tired  was.

She could scarcely sit upright on the

 .

Then at last 's luck changed.

A kind-hearted offered them

his stable. Thankfully  accepted.

The stable was warm and the

animals there, the big heavy

and the sleepy  , were quiet and

friendly.

That night  Jesus was born

and  wrapped him in

swaddling clothes.  filled the

 with clean straw so that

could lay him there.

In the morning some  came

to the stable. When they saw the

 in the , wrapped in

swaddling clothes, they were filled

with joy. "It is just as the

said," one  whispered. "He is

Christ the Lord!"

A bright new  in the East

was a sign to three  that a new

 had been born.

The  followed the

through many lands until, at last,

they found the  Jesus in

Bethlehem. They bowed low before

him and offered the  the

they had chosen to be fit for a great

 . Then they mounted their

 and rode swiftly away back to

their own land.

 did not take his little family back to Nazareth. Instead he took the  and his mother to Egypt where they would be safe from the wicked Herod.

Herod had tried to find the holy child so that he could have him killed. But  had been warned in a dream to leave

Bethlehem before Herod's

could discover where they lived.

When the wicked  died they

went back to Nazareth.

 grew up in Nazareth. He

went to school like the other boys

and when he was grown-up he

became a carpenter like  .

Sometimes  talked to the

 on the shore of the Lake of

Galilee.  told them about the

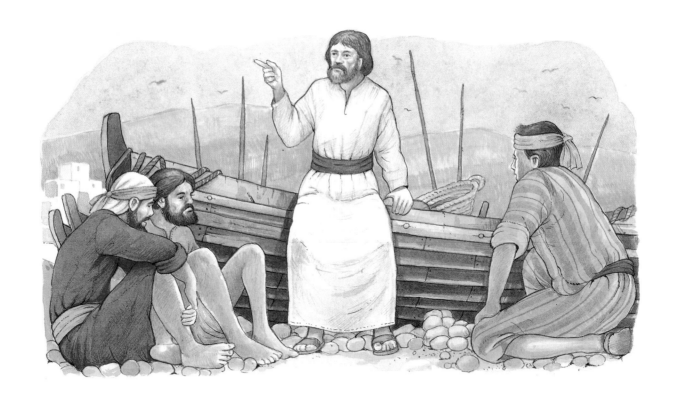

Kingdom of Heaven as they sat by

their mending their  .

Two of the  were brothers.

They wanted very much to try and

be like  . "We will follow you,"

they said. And they left their

and their  and followed him.

One  who loved  was

Peter. He went everywhere with

. Once he joined a great crowd

of people who had come to hear

 speak. The people would not

go home even though they were tired

and hungry.  took a little boy's

supper of two and some small

 and suddenly there was

enough food to feed all the people.

No wonder Peter was astonished!

There was even enough  left

over to fill twelve  .

Sometimes  talked about

going to heaven. He told Peter and

his friends that he would not be with

them for long.

The day came when  said he

must go to Jerusalem and his friends

found a  for him to ride. The

crowds were so happy to see
they waved  in the air and
greeted him with shouts of joy. But

 had enemies in Jerusalem who were plotting to kill him.

That same week  came to the quiet little garden where  was praying. The  took him away and put him in prison. His enemies saw to it that  was sentenced to die on the

The day died on the

was a sad day for Peter and his

friends. But  did not leave

them for long. He came down from

heaven to be with them again for a

short time, filling their hearts with

joy and happiness.